American Sailing Ships
Coloring Book

by PETER F. COPELAND

DOVER PUBLICATIONS, INC., New York

Introduction

THE HISTORY OF American sailing ships began with the first settlers who arrived on our shores. The early colonists could not have survived in the trackless wilderness without some means of transportation, so ship- and boatbuilders were among the earliest craftsmen to practice their art in Colonial America.

American sailing-ship builders and seamen proved themselves to be among the finest the world had ever seen during those proud years when the Stars and Stripes, seen flying from a mizzen truck, proclaimed a ship to be a Yankee clipper—one of the fastest, cleanest, hardest-driven ships in the world.

Today's yachtsmen and sports sailors keep the art and lore of the sailing ship alive in such pageants as the Tall Ships Race, begun in 1976, in which many of the world's surviving deep-sea sailing ships gather to remind us of another, more romantic, time.

This book is a picture history of American sailing vessels, showing the little shallow-draft topsail schooners of Colonial times, the fighting frigates and privateers of our early wars, the clippers, early sail-and-steam-powered vessels, fishing boats and yachts, the working schooners at the end of the age of sail, a few survivors and a reconstruction built in our own time. The year in parentheses at the end of the first phrase of each caption indicates the date of the view shown.

Over the course of many years spent at sea, it was my good fortune to have served, albeit briefly, on two sailing ships. One of them—the *Gazella Primeiro,* on which I served as boatswain during a brief voyage in 1974—is shown on page 43.

PETER F. COPELAND

To Kent and Maria

Published in Canada by General Publishing Company, Ltd.,
30 Lesmill Road, Don Mills, Toronto, Ontario.
Published in the United Kingdom by Constable and Company, Ltd.

American Sailing Ships Coloring Book is a new work, first published by Dover Publications, Inc., in 1987.

DOVER *Pictorial Archive* SERIES

International Standard Book Number: 0-486-25388-0

Manufactured in the United States of America
Dover Publications, Inc.
31 East 2nd Street
Mineola, N.Y. 11501

The privateer frigate *Bethel* **(1748).** Frigates were speedy vessels and made efficient ships of war. The square-rigged *Bethel* was large for her time. An armed wartime commerce raider, she captured a Spanish treasure ship in 1748.

A Colonial sloop (1760). Most Colonial sailing vessels were smaller than their European contemporaries. The sloop rig seen here was popular, as were other schooner rigs (vessels with fore and aft sails). They were cheap to build and more economical to operate than the larger, square-rigged European vessels.

The schooner *Sultana* (1768). This ship is a good example of a small American trading vessel of Colonial times. All merchant ships of the period were armed; the *Sultana* carried small swivel guns that could be mounted upon her bulwarks. She was purchased by the British government for use in the Royal Navy in 1768.

The Continental schooner *Hannah* **(1775).** New Englanders claim that the *Hannah* was the first armed ship in the service of the Colonies during the American Revolution. In September 1775 she captured the British ship *Unity* and brought her into Gloucester, Massachusetts. The *Hannah* is seen here evading the shot of a large British cruiser.

The privateer brig *Montgomery* **(1776).** In July 1776 the 18-gun ship, out of Philadelphia, captured the *Millern,* an English merchant ship, off the coast of Ireland. Shortly afterward she was herself captured by the British. In August 1776 she was recaptured by the American privateer Oliver Cromwell and taken into Boston.

The Continental frigate *Randolph* (1776). During the summer of 1777, the fast 32-gun *Randolph*, commanded by Captain Nicholas Biddle, took four prizes, which she delivered at Charleston, South Carolina. A Pennsylvania-built ship, she was blown up in battle with the British 64-gun H.M.S. *Yarmouth* off Barbados in 1778.

The Continental Navy brig *Andrew Doria* (1776). The ship began life as a merchantman, but was purchased for the Continental service in 1775, at the outset of the American Revolution. She was armed with 14 four-pound guns. To avoid capture by the British, her own crew burned her in the Delaware River in 1777.

The gunboat *Philadelphia* (1776). Designed by Benedict Arnold for the defense of the northern frontier during the American Revolution, the *Philadelphia* was one of eight gunboats built on Lake Champlain. She was sunk at the battle of Valcour Island in October 1776. In 1935, the *Philadelphia* was raised from the bottom of the lake and today may be seen, much as she appeared in 1776, at the Smithsonian Institution's National Museum of American History in Washington, D.C. In the background is the Continental schooner *Revenge*.

The Continental sloop of war *Ranger* (1777). The 18-gun ship was built at Portsmouth, New Hampshire, in 1777. Captain John Paul Jones sailed her out of the port of Nantes, France, in February 1778, receiving the first salute to the flag of the new United States by a foreign government. The *Ranger* was captured by the British at Charleston, South Carolina, in 1780 and was taken into the Royal Navy.

The Continental galley-frigate *Confederacy* (1778). The unlucky *Confederacy* was built at Norwich, Connecticut. Bigger than a British 36-gun frigate of the time (though she mounted the same number of guns), she was captured by the British off the Virginia Capes in 1781 and was taken into the service of the Royal Navy.

The frigate *South Carolina* **(1781).** The largest frigate to fly the American flag during the Revolution, she had been built in Amsterdam and eventually entered the service of the South Carolina State Navy. In her first five days at sea as a ship of war she took five British ships and in 1782 participated in the American capture of Nassau, in the Bahamas. The 40-gun frigate was captured by three British ships after a fierce fight off the Delaware River in 1782.

A Chebacco boat (1810). The Chebacco boat was a development of the old double shallop, used in the coastal fisheries of Colonial New England. This 40-foot boat was popular among northern fishermen for many years, from the late eighteenth century till long after the War of 1812.

The U.S.S. *Constitution* battles H.M.S. *Guerrière* (1812). In August 1812 the 44-gun frigate *Constitution* defeated and burned the *Guerrière* in what is perhaps the best-remembered sea battle of our second war with Great Britain. Launched in 1797, the *Constitution* ("Old Ironsides") survives to this day, on view in Boston harbor, as the Navy's oldest ship in active commission.

The privateer schooner *Rambler* (1812). The *Rambler* belonged to a unique class of American sailing ships known as "schooner clippers" or "hermaphrodite schooners." They were fast, maneuverable vessels that made excellent commerce raiders in wartime.

The Baltimore clipper schooner *Chasseur* **(1813).** This famous privateer brig was built in Baltimore in 1813. She mounted 14 guns and was brilliantly successful as a commerce raider in the War of 1812. The Baltimore clippers were modified Chesapeake Bay coastal trading schooners.

A U.S. Revenue Marine cutter (1815). The U.S. Revenue Marine, an ancestor of the modern U.S. Coast Guard, employed fast schooners, or cutters like the 51-ton cutter seen here, in such services as the suppression of the slave trade and piracy, lifesaving duties, carrying dispatches and assisting the Navy in wartime.

The yacht *Cleopatra's Barge* **(1816).** The first American yacht to cross the Atlantic, she sailed around Europe and later went to the Pacific, where she became the private yacht of the king of Hawaii.

The paddle steamer sailing packet *Savannah* (1819). The 380-ton *Savannah* began life as a sailing vessel but was fitted out with a steam engine and paddle wheels that could be folded up and laid on deck when not in use. In 1819 the ship made maritime history by becoming the first steam-powered vessel to cross the Atlantic (though she was, in fact, under sail for most of the voyage).

The schooner *Union* (1823). This American-built vessel, used at one time as a slaver, was one of the earliest schooners to employ pivoted centerboards that extended below the keel to achieve stability when sailing to windward.

19

A hermaphrodite brig (1830). The hermaphrodite, or half-brig, was a popular American sailing vessel in the nineteenth century. Of its two masts, the fore was square-rigged; the second, or mainmast, was schooner-rigged with fore and aft sails.

The schooner *Dos Amigos* (1832). This Baltimore-built slave ship was captured by the British slave-patrol ship *Black Joke* in 1832 and was taken into the Royal Navy to be used to help stamp out the illegal African slave trade.

The ship-sloop *Vincennes* **(1838).** One of 11 ship-sloops built for the Navy between 1825 and 1830, the *Vincennes* was the flagship of the Wilkes Exploring Expedition, in which six vessels explored and charted the islands of the Pacific, Antarctica, the Straits of Magellan and the Northwest coast of the United States.

The clipper ship *Helena* (1849). American shipbuilders designed and built the fastest clipper ships that ever sailed in response to the demand by Gold Rush adventurers for fast passage from the Eastern United States to California around Cape Horn.

A Nantucket whaler (1850). For over 100 years, the Yankee whalers of New England ranged the oceans of the world, hunting and killing whales and loading their ships with casks of whale oil. Here a whaleboat pulls after a whale. The harpooner in the bow of the boat levels his weapon to plunge it into the whale.

The clipper ship *Flying Cloud* (1851). Built for the California trade spawned by the Gold Rush of 1849, the *Flying Cloud,* one of the finest and fastest of the great clippers built and designed by the famous Donald McKay, was one of the few sailing vessels in history to sail more than 400 sea miles in a single 24-hour period.

The Great Lakes schooner *Challenge* **(1852).** Early in America's history, the Great Lakes became a route for transporting the ore and lumber located in the interior of the country. By the late nineteenth century, merchant vessels of the Great Lakes were carrying cargoes equal to America's entire foreign commerce. Most Great Lakes schooners were shallow-draft, gracefully slim vessels, able to navigate the canals of the lakes' transportation systems.

The clipper ship *Lightning* **(1854).** The ship was designed by Donald McKay and built in Boston for the Australian trade. The age of the clipper ship has been called "the most remarkable ten years of sail in the history of the world." These fast, lean square-riggers were the finest sailing ships ever built.

The clipper ship *Andrew Jackson* (1855). This medium clipper, built in 1855, almost equaled the famed *Flying Cloud*'s record 89-day passage from the Eastern United States to San Francisco around Cape Horn.

The packet ship *James Foster, Jr.* (1855). The Black Ball Line, begun in 1818, established the first regularly scheduled sailing-ship service between the United States and foreign ports. Sailing out of New York, the packet-ship companies (Black Ball, Red Star and Swallowtail lines) helped to establish the city as the nation's leading seaport.

C.S.S. *Alabama* (1864). The Confederate commerce raider *Alabama*, a 1000-ton vessel cruising under steam and sail, took 66 Union merchant ships in two years of wartime operation. Here, in one of the most memorable sea fights of the Civil War, she was sunk by the warship U.S.S. *Kearsarge* off Cherbourg, France.

U.S.S. _Hartford_ (1864). The steam sloop _Hartford_ was Admiral David Farragut's flagship in July 1864, at the Battle of Mobile Bay, during which the ship was repeatedly struck and took heavy casualties. Farragut climbed into the port main shrouds and remained in this exposed position to observe the battle.

The merchant ship *Mary Celeste* (1872). In November 1872 the *Mary Celeste* left New York, bound for Genoa, Italy, with a cargo of alcohol. Eight days later a Nova Scotia brig discovered her, under sail in mid-ocean, completely deserted. The captain, his wife and daughter and a crew of seven men had disappeared. No trace of them, nor explanation of their fate, has ever been found.

The pilot schooner *Hesper* **(1884).** Built in 1884 in Boston, the boat was thought to be the fastest pilot schooner of her time. The model for many Massachusetts-built fishing schooners, she became a yacht when she was finally sold by the Boston Pilots Association. She was broken up in 1912.

The yacht *America* (1885). The big surprise of the British Cowes Yacht Race of 1851 was the speedy yacht *America*, entered by the New York Yacht Club, which won so decisively that she left her British competitors out of sight.

The coasting schooner *King Philip* (1886). This fine-looking four-masted schooner was built at Camden, Maine, in 1886. In 1892 she was one of a number of big schooners in the coal trade, hauling cargoes from Newport News and Norfolk, Virginia, to Portsmouth, New Hampshire, and Fall River, Massachusetts.

The stone schooner *Annie and Reuben* **(1891).** In common with many schooners involved in the coastal trade between East Coast ports around the turn of the century, the *Annie and Reuben* hauled bulk cargoes, in this case stone. She was built in 1891 at Bath, Maine.

The two-masted schooner *Harriet C. Whitehead* **(1892).** Built at Waterford, Connecticut, in 1892 the ship spent most of her working life on Chesapeake Bay, and was still sailing in the 1920s. At 211 tons, she ranked among the heaviest two-masted schooners.

The Friendship sloop *Black Jack* **(1900).** The first Friendship sloop was built in 1875 as a lobsterman's workboat. These fast, trim, Maine-built schooners soon became a favorite of yachtsmen. Several hundred were built between 1890 and 1915. A few remain in existence today.

The bark *Foohng Suey* (1903). Successors to the wooden clipper ships of the 1850s were the last of the square-rigged merchant sailers—steel-built barks like the *Foohng Suey*—that could compete with steamships only by carrying low-paying bulk cargoes such as nitrate and coal. Among the last square-riggers under the United States flag were the "Star" ships of the Alaska Packers Association, which carried men and supplies to the Alaska salmon canneries as late as 1930.

The seven-masted schooner *Thomas W. Lawson* (1907). Because American schooners were among the most economical sailing vessels in the world, even in the twilight of the age of the sailing ship (1910–25), there were still many working schooners at sea. The *Thomas W. Lawson* was the only seven-masted schooner ever built. She was lost off the coast of England on her first deep-water voyage, broken up on the reefs of the Scilly Isles in a great storm.

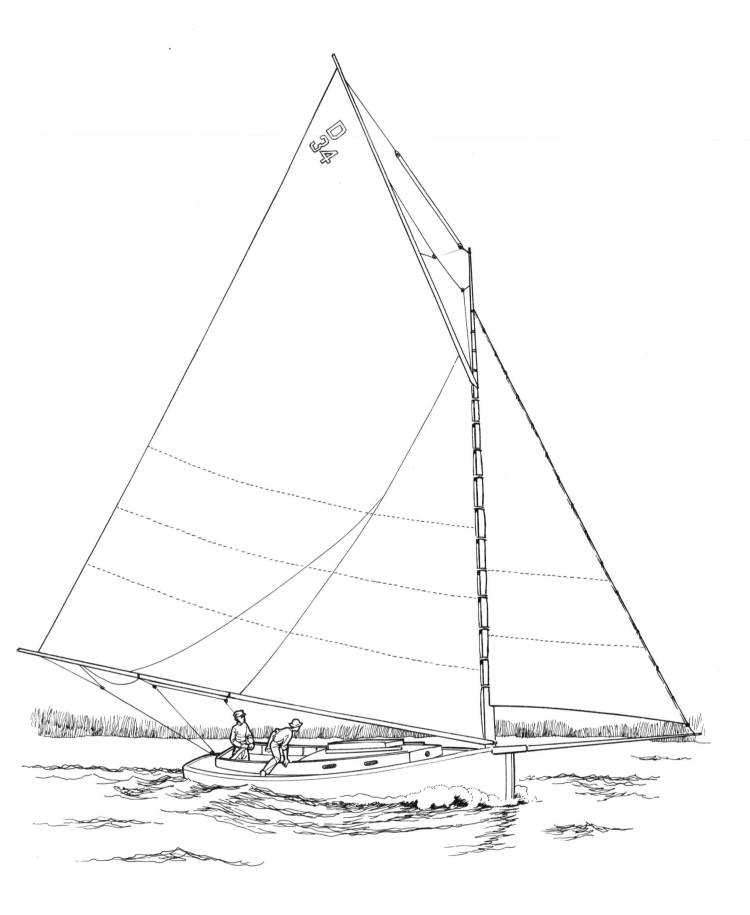

The catboat *Iris* (1908). The uniquely American catboat has been built and sailed all along the Northeast Coast of the United States from Cape Cod to Barnegat Bay. Originally a working fishing boat, it became popular with sport sailors and has been built as a pleasure craft for over 80 years. The *Iris* won the Massachusetts Bay championship race in 1908.

The schooner *Lois M. Candage* (1912). The ship was typical of the New England working schooner still commonly seen in the early years of this century. She was built at Blue Hill, Maine, in 1912 and was still afloat, in Camden, Maine, in the early 1950s, taking sightseers on tourist cruises.

The barkentine *Gazella Primeiro* **(1974).** In 1970 the Philadelphia Maritime Museum purchased this Portuguese barkentine, which was then the oldest wooden sailing vessel still in active service. She was launched in 1883 and, it is said, sailed as a whaleship, a cargo carrier and, for the last 70 years of her life, as a Grand Banks fisherman.

U.S. Coast Guard training ship *Eagle* (1976). Manned by Coast Guard cadets, each summer the *Eagle* sails from New London, Connecticut, on Atlantic training cruises. She regularly takes part in the famous Tall Ships Race, competing against other surviving sailing ships from Europe and South America.

The pinnace *Dove* (1986). In the past 20 years, various American historical institutions have produced replicas of certain historic vessels of the seventeenth century that were involved in the establishment of early settlements in North America. The *Dove*, built on Maryland's Eastern Shore and launched in 1978, is a recreation of one of the ships that carried the colonists of Lord Baltimore to the New World in 1633 and helped establish the settlement at St. Marys City, Maryland's first capital.